C000241569

THE KATHLEEN PARTRIDGE SERIES

Kathleen Partridge's Book of Flowers
Kathleen Partridge's Book of Friendship
Kathleen Partridge's Book of Golden Thoughts
Kathleen Partridge's Book of Tranquil Moments
Kathleen Partridge's Book of Faith
Kathleen Partridge's Book of Happiness
Kathleen Partridge's Book of Seasons
Kathleen Partridge's Book of Hope

First published in Great Britain in 1997 by
Jarrold Publishing Ltd
Whitefriars, Norwich NR3 1TR

Designed and produced by Visual Image, Craigend, Brimley Hill,
Churchstanton, Taunton, Somerset TA3 7QH

Illustrations by Jane Watkins

Edited by Donald Greig

ISBN 0-7117-0971-8

Printed by Proost, Belgium 1/97

$\mathcal{K}$athleen $\mathcal{P}$artridge's
BOOK OF
$Happiness$

Kathleen Partridge

The Daily Round

A friend who comes to visit you,
A friend to go and see,
A round of worthwhile duty
And some leisure, duty free.
A hobby to pick up again,
A good book to begin,
A merry evening out,
A quiet evening staying in.
A time for carefree laughter
And for peaceful contemplation,
For music to your heart's desire
And quiet conversation.
These things make up the balance
Of a pleasant daily round,
What more is there to do?
What greater pleasure can be found?

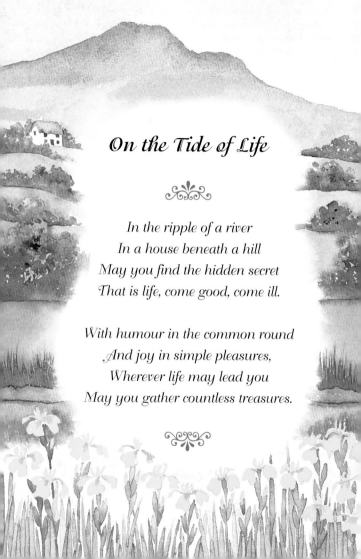

On the Tide of Life

In the ripple of a river
In a house beneath a hill
May you find the hidden secret
That is life, come good, come ill.

With humour in the common round
And joy in simple pleasures,
Wherever life may lead you
May you gather countless treasures.

Thinking of You

May you soon be walking
In the meadows cool and green,
Breathing scent and sunshine
Where the landscape is serene.

May you soon be laughing
With your family and friends,
Visiting and entertaining
When this ordeal ends.

Singing while you work
The way you do, and sharing fun
While giving joy to other folk
As you have always done.

Tune of the Day

A joyful manner of living
Is a tune for the day to start,
The pleasure in doing and giving
Brings peace to the happy heart.

With courage for daily duty
And patience when problems arise,
Thankful for bounty and beauty
Living in ways that are wise.

Far Away Places

Turn back the page, the page of time
To the olden days of maypoles and mime,
To a white horse carved on an old green hill
With a mason's art and a carpenter's skill.

To beautiful churches in ancient glory
And stained glass windows that tell a story,
Turn back the page, recapture grace
And try to live at a quieter pace.

Wisdom of the Waves

When the ships are safe in harbour
And the boats are anchored tight
When the sun gleams on the water
There is not a fairer sight.

The lonely heart is comforted
The troubled mind set free
As if the cares of all the world
Were sailing out to sea.

Another Day

Old cares are like the morning mist
Before the rising sun,
But it is true, the blue shines through
Before the day is done.

And then the fears of yesteryears
Go rolling down the lane,
Another day, smiles on its way
And life begins again.

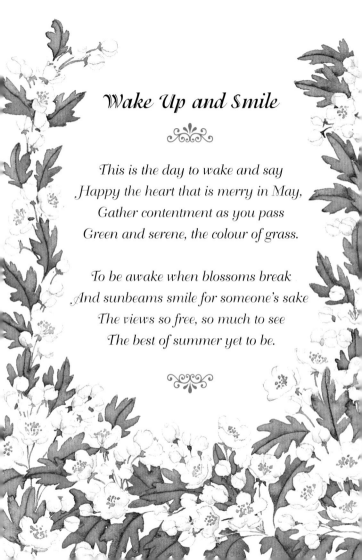

Wake Up and Smile

This is the day to wake and say
Happy the heart that is merry in May,
Gather contentment as you pass
Green and serene, the colour of grass.

To be awake when blossoms break
And sunbeams smile for someone's sake
The views so free, so much to see
The best of summer yet to be.

The Old Home

The curtains may be fading from the shade
they were when new,
The carpets getting threadbare, the
upholstery wearing through;
But what a grand and happy home these
items represent,
A story goes to every patch, a memoir to
each rent.
The years of wear were family fun and
generous entertaining,
The beauty of the home is dulled, the
welcome still remaining;
And it will serve the parents and their family
and friends
For many years and dearer grow with every
year that ends.

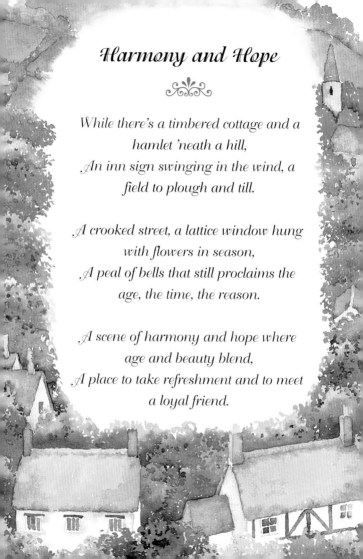

Harmony and Hope

While there's a timbered cottage and a
hamlet 'neath a hill,
An inn sign swinging in the wind, a
field to plough and till.

A crooked street, a lattice window hung
with flowers in season,
A peal of bells that still proclaims the
age, the time, the reason.

A scene of harmony and hope where
age and beauty blend,
A place to take refreshment and to meet
a loyal friend.

A cosy room, a shelf of books to make a leisured choice
While waiting for a simple meal and well-beloved voice.

While there's a spire against the sky and cattle idly grazing,
There will be peace within the heart that finds the time for lazing.

Teasing

The nicest homes are those where people love to tease
each other –
Good-tempered sort of banter of a sister to a brother;
The chaffing and the laughing of a husband with a
wife,
Making happy fun out of the ups and downs of life.

The joking and the raillery on which good cheer
attends,
Between the next-door neighbours, or the home
that's shared by friends;
For loving goes with teasing, 'tis the heart's way of
protection,
And such a very happy way of showing fond
affection.

Easy Asset

The common zest of living
Is a most infectious thing,
Happiness is catching,
Laughter has an echoing ring.
So even if our knowledge
Isn't brilliant or excessive,
Our wit not very funny
Nor our character impressive –

Yet good spirits and a zest for life
Will take us anywhere,
We may not have a lot to spend
But we've good cheer to spare.
Such an easy asset,
Like a banner kept unfurled,
And then at least we bring
A little joy into the world.

Happy Hill

❧❧❧

I planted not one blade of grass upon
this happy hill,
And yet may wander in and out the
buttercups at will.

I offered nothing to promote the
growth of any tree,
And yet they give their shelter and
their majesty to me.

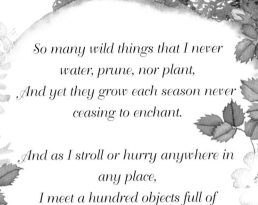

So many wild things that I never
water, prune, nor plant,
And yet they grow each season never
ceasing to enchant.

And as I stroll or hurry anywhere in
any place,
I meet a hundred objects full of
loveliness and grace.

They are not yours nor mine, that
cheer the day and scent the air,
But we are privileged to look upon
them and to share.

Listening

When hearing the birds sing,
I always imagine that theirs is a life of contentment
and joy;
That they are so happy, untrammelled and carefree,
Without any problems to irk and annoy.

But maybe they, too, have their setbacks and
sorrows,
Maybe their infants are quarrelsome, too;
A nest leaks, their food could be sometimes more
varied,
Or they feel the cold when the sky isn't blue.

But we'd never guess from their bright little manners
And we'd never know from the sound of their song,
They always seem happy and lively and busy
And sing just as sweetly the whole daytime long.

The Picnic

Maybe the kettle takes longer to boil
And the ground isn't soft as a chair,
Maybe the butter runs soft in the sun
And the cake seems to wilt in the air.

Maybe a wasp drowns himself in the jam
And the leaves float on top of the tea,
And maybe you get a bit cramped in your foot
When you balance a plate on your knee.

But you eat from a table the whole long year round,
Politely, from Jan. to December,
While a meal in the open air loosens your laugh
And is always a joy to remember.

Joy of Living

Above the lapping ocean, where the gulls are flying high,
Is the freedom of the firmament and wisdom of the sky.

In the bosom of the billows, that have rocked the stars to rest,
The purpose of existence overall is manifest.

For what is more important, when a gull is flying free,
Than the majesty of life above the vast expanse of sea?

Ambition simply satisfied to glory and to give
In exhilarating movement just to breathe, to eat, to live.

The high ambitions of mankind, for grandeur, gold and greed,
Against the beauty of the scene look very small indeed.